MEMBERS OF THE TRIBE

MEMBERS OF THE
TRIBE

CARICATURES OF GAY MEN AND LESBIANS BY
MICHAEL WILLHOITE

ALYSON PUBLICATIONS

Typeset and printed in the United States of America.

Published by Alyson Publications, Inc.,
40 Plympton Street, Boston, Massachusetts 02118.
Distributed in England by GMP Publishers,
P.O. Box 247, London N17 9QR, England.

First edition: November 1993

2 4 5 3 1

ISBN 1-55583-238-5

Library of Congress Cataloging-in-Publication Data

Willhoite, Michael, 1946–
    Members of the tribe : caricatures of gay men and lesbians / by
Michael Willhoite. — 1st ed.
        p.   cm.
    Includes index.
    ISBN 1-55583-238-5 : $24.95
        1. Gay men—Biography.   2. Gay men—Caricatures and cartoons.
3. Lesbians—Biography.   4. Lesbians—Caricatures and cartoons.
I. Title.
HQ75.7.W55 1993
305.38'9664—dc20   93-29577
                                                                        CIP

CONTENTS

h, Michael!" My friend's face opened up like a peony when I told her about *Members of the Tribe*. "A book about Jewish people!" I hated to disappoint her, but a collection of Jewish caricatures will have to wait. This book celebrates a different tribe.

One dictionary definition of a tribe is: a collection of people with a common interest, habit, or occupation. So, do gay men and lesbians constitute a tribe? Wildly diverse, we would seem to have little in common except an excessive fondness for our own sex, as the most cursory skimming of *Members of the Tribe* will demonstrate. I mean, imagine a dinner party composed of Peter Allen, Lizzie Borden, J. Edgar Hoover, Lillian Hellman, Charles Ludlam, and Martina Navratilova. Why, you wouldn't get past the salad before the fur flew!

So "tribe" is a convenience. For years I've asked friends about one person or another in the public eye, "Is he a ... (coy pause) member of our tribe?" OK, so it's a little disingenuous, a bit cute. But so is "a friend of Dorothy." But hell, we're cute people. (Wait — Roy Cohn, *cute*? There. That's what I mean about our diversity.)

With a few exceptions, these drawings first appeared in the pages of the *Washington Blade*, the best gay newspaper in the nation (in this artist's opinion). Each was accompanied by a brief bio, and celebrated a birthday — at first. Given scheduling difficulties (gay people adamantly refused to be born some weeks), I later added death dates. Then an occasional special day, like a stage debut or some other. For this book, I was able to dispense with the dating framework. These people are simply here because they're here. Or rather, because they're queer.

Some are not even that. Many of my subjects have been — or claimed to be — bisexual. A few folks merely experimented. I was even able to portray the august and manifestly straight Winston Churchill (in the *Blade* but not here) because he claimed to have tried it once, with actor Ivor Novello. And some are here by the grace of the Rumor That Refuses to Die People have always asked me, how do you find out who's gay? Easy. I'm a wide-ranging, voracious reader. Every time I come across some information I can use in this line, I inscribe the name (and those pesky dates) in a red notebook. I consider one printed reference enough. The nasty tabloids whose headlines trumpet their scandals at one in the supermarket line have often sent me in the direction of research. I DO NOT READ THOSE RAGS, let me hasten to add. But, hey, while your ice cream melts and the gabby matron ahead of you can't find her coupons, one *can* peek...

Some of my drawings have been used as illustrations for other books under the Alyson imprint, and fifty-three of the little darlings appeared in my 1990 *Gay Desk Calendar.* Only a couple are duplicated here. Some are brand-new. The recent disclosures about that fun-loving old queen J. Edgar called for a new, more savage caricature than the previous rather sober — and kind — drawing. I fell to it, you can imagine, with fiendish glee.

It will be immediately apparent that I like to draw. I also like to change drawing styles frequently. Nothing bores me quite so thoroughly as seeing drawing after plodding drawing in the same technique (the sublime Hirschfeld being a glorious exception). My favorite caricaturist is Max Beerbohm, who danced like a dragonfly from style to style, as his subject dictated, so I have taken him as a guide. He executed all his drawings from memory, which I've been unable to do, Julius Caesar, for example, being hard to pin down to an appointment.

Some of my subjects have seen their caricatures and have reacted variously. Emlyn Williams, the actor-playwright, was immensely pleased by his. James Ivory bought my caricature of Ismail Merchant for his friend's birthday. *That* gave me an inordinate amount of pleasure, you can be sure. But a certain author, I heard by the grapevine, threatened to have my *cojones* on a stake — not because of the drawing, a pleasant piece of work, but because I had revealed her age! Ah, well, I'm glad Murad IV missed his portrait here (by several centuries); his retribution might have been even more terrible. My *cojones*, by the way, remain intact.

After a decade of doing caricatures for the *Washington Blade*, I still haven't run out of fresh subjects. Gays and lesbians, bless us, keep pouring out of the closet. Some choice subjects are still burrowed into theirs; I'll simply have to wait. And oh, how I *long* to get my nib into a few folks! Not until that recent book could I put J. Edgar Hoover into garter belt and fishnet stockings. Wouldn't it be a delight to get old Jesse Helms onto illustration board? I can see him now: in a frilly pink dress, a bow affixed to his remaining wisps of hair, singing — à la Baby Jane — "I've Written a Letter to Dad-dy." One lives in eternal hope...

I'm deeply grateful to many people. My friends and adorable family have been supportive and loving from the first. Don Michaels of the *Washington Blade* first took a chance on me in 1979, and continues as a Presence in my professional life. Sasha Alyson has re-published my caricatures and given me the chance to write and illustrate children's books like *Daddy's Roommate.* And very special thanks to Michael Himovitz, of Sacramento. He gave me my first gallery showing, a *major* high, and Jane Fonda sponsored it as an AIDS benefit. I'm endlessly grateful to both of them. I owe a special debt to that good old American institution, the public library. Several in Massachusetts — Framingham, Natick, Newton, and especially Wellesley — have been crucial to my research. Wellesley's has been a second home.

And thanks to all you brave souls who make my job so much easier by being out of the closet. Even if you've been *yanked* out. To those remaining within, I encourage you to come out and breathe the free air. You'll love it.

—MICHAEL WILLHOITE

To Darling Dana,
for more reasons than I can
fit on this page.

To some of us, the voice of the sixties was not the Beatles. It was a golden ribbon floating out of the throat of Joan Baez, and its purity is undiminished today. She was pure of purpose too, a folksinger who embraced one cause after another. The centerpiece was, of course, opposition to the Vietnam War, which dominated all our lives then. The Newport Folk Festival made her a name, but Woodstock made her a legend. Though she had a turbulent love affair with the young Bob Dylan, she married anti-war activist David Harris. It didn't last, but resulted in a beloved son, Gabriel. She writes of all this — and of a love affair with another woman — in her book *And a Voice to Sing With.*

kay. You're the man who has everything: inherited wealth, energy to spare for work *and* fun. The name Malcolm Forbes is known everywhere. You are a champion hot-air balloonist; editor-in-chief of that bible of capitalism, *Forbes Magazine;* the owner of chateaux and palaces, yachts and jets, and scores of motorcycles. And let's not forget that twelve-thousand-bottle wine cellar. You can ball any young man you want to lay hands on (an invitation to the sauna is a favorite ploy). You're *very* well known in New York's seedy downtown biker bars and the gutter press presses closer. You need a beard. Hey! how about a great sex symbol for company? ... Liz Taylor, say...?

Families, and the cutthroat struggles for power within them, are the subject of the twenty-two novels of Ivy Compton-Burnett (rhymes with "turn it"). She gathered material from her own family, whom she regarded with a cold loathing, and whom she neatly replaced with one soul: Margaret Jourdain. The books all teach the same lesson: never turn your back. Each is set in a Victorian household governed by a tyrant. Each is composed almost entirely of malicious, martini-dry conversations, with only brief scraps of narration or description. Masters and servants, children and adults all speak in the same dry epigrammatical mode. Nobody wrote novels even *remotely* like them.

Graceful prose, good talk, alcohol, and — rather more disastrously — rough trade: these were a few of the favorite things of James Pope-Hennessy (forget raindrops on roses and whiskers on kittens). A difficult, rebellious youth provided him with a questing mind and a deep sympathy for the underdog. He wrote history and biographies, with a highly descriptive, almost poetic writing style. In early 1974 he was eager to begin a new biography of Noel Coward, for which he received a large advance. But he indiscreetly mentioned this sum to a couple of hunks-for-hire he had invited to his maisonette for a little of the down and dirty. And they blithely murdered him for it.

Really, now. Does *anybody* disagree with Ruth Benedict that the potlatching Kwakiutl provide a parody on our own economic arrangements? Well? No, I didn't think so ... Benedict was a pioneering anthropologist, and the product of a Baptist childhood who found a truer light in her study of American Indian religion. Her *Patterns of Culture* is a classic work that still arouses heated debate among anthropologists, but *The Chrysanthemum and the Sword*, written during wartime as a study of our "most alien enemy," was so very on-the-mark that it was a revelation even to its subject, the Japanese. Benedict was emotionally aloof all her life, except to Ruth Valentine, in whose arms she died.

his terrible Turk is Murad IV, a remorseless meanie if ever there was one. The last warrior-sultan of the Ottoman Empire, he succeeded his mad uncle Mustafa I, and proceeded to wreak havoc with, shall we say, excessive gusto. Mutilation and dismemberment were two of his favorite methods of maintaining order. Not above ordering, as casually as one would a pizza, the deaths of family members, he did have a fugitive capacity for love, or at least buggery. One of his young Turkish delights was captured and, well, *shared* liberally. Murad's response was a carnival of butchery. Vengeance is mine! — or, hell, maybe it was just his idea of fun.

Superb critic and essayist, founder and editor of *Horizon*, Cyril Connolly was an indefatigable man of letters. His body of literary essays are unsurpassed for their exuberance and readability. Connolly's great theme was the danger of early success ("whom the gods would destroy, they first call promising"), but it was a strange judgment to make upon himself. His last book, *The Evening Colonnade*, was a collection of essays, and as masterful as his early work. Like many "straight" public-school Britons, he spent a highly industrious adolescence pouncing his schoolmates. Not a happy man, taken altogether, though he got much solace from food, wine, and the adoration of his many friends.

All together now, a rousing chorus of "I Enjoy Being a Girl." Poor J. Edgar Hoover! All those years of pretending *so hard* to be a big tough G-man, when all the time — gulp! — he was starring in his own clandestine production of *La Cage aux Folles*. And for an audience of one: his dough-faced main squeeze, Clyde Tolson (another ersatz toughie). Not only do we now know the FBI director to have been in the mob's pocket, but it seems that he was the ultimate closet queen and a hypocrite's hypocrite besides. (His intense homophobia was obviously the rage of Caliban at seeing his own face in the mirror.) Poor man ... when you look like a bull-dog's butt, the loveliest gown can only do *so much*.

rue romantics are advised to stop reading right here. Mata Hari, the exotic dancer and World War I spy, was not quite the romantic legend that history has dished up, but rather a decidedly plump and dowdy young Dutchwoman. An early marriage to a dull soldier soon degenerated into mutual loathing, and they parted. Three years later, art modeling not paying *terribly* well, she burst on Paris as Mata Hari. (Which fit better on a marquee than Margaretha Geertruida Zelle MacLeod.) She pursued a nice sideline as a courtesan — and dabbled in women too — but the legend really took flight when the French shot her as a spy. Trouble is, she probably wasn't guilty of much more than indiscreet blabbing, which landed her in the *potage.*

19

Zora Neale Hurston's spirit always got her in trouble. Her father, a Baptist preacher, was threatened by her independence, sassiness, and bright inquisitive mind. But you can't keep a good girl down, and she escaped her hometown of Eatonville, Florida, as a lady's maid with a Gilbert and Sullivan troupe — hey, by any means necessary, right? A couple of marriages didn't pan out, but her writing did. *Their Eyes Were Watching God* was her greatest novel, but she also wrote the classic of black folklore, *Mules and Men.* Unfortunately, Hurston peaked early. Quarrels with her many mentors and an increasing conservatism dragged her down and she died destitute — even her gravesite isn't known exactly. But the books are indelible.

The stud/ious gentlemen above are both Samuel M. Steward, a literary chameleon *par excellence*. He was an intimate friend of Gertrude Stein and Alice B. Toklas, and published a selection of their letters to him, along with a memoir. He has also written a series of witty erotic novels under the name Phil Andros (note the pun, students), short stories in the hundreds, and more-traditional novels. He has even contributed — are you ready for this? — to the *Illinois Dental Journal* and *The World Book Encyclopedia*, and worked as a tattoo artist. His bibliographer has his work cut out for him — Sam's written under at least ten pseudonyms.

ane Bowles produced a mere handful of work, but choice stuff, indeed. Collected, it fills one manageable volume: *My Sister's Hand in Mine.* Mostly her influence was as a friend to such writers as Truman Capote and Tennessee Williams, and as the wife of composer-writer Paul Bowles. Marginally a feminist, she wrote of women, not issues, and with great style. Alas, she was a prize neurotic. She managed to stave off loneliness in a series of failed affairs with women, but not even the springs of love could water her talent. In North Africa, in her later years, a crippling writer's block edged her into madness. And she died, thoroughly broken, at fifty-six.

William John Cook of London's working-class East End christened himself Antony Tudor, a more fitting name, he thought, to conquer the world of ballet. A dancer at first, he very early decided to be a creator rather than an interpreter. He would be a choreographer, and America was the sphere in which he chose to work. In the words of his friendly rival Agnes De Mille, "What he asked for was magic, and he got it." His muse was ballerina Nora Kaye, but his lover (for 54 years) was dark, gorgeous Hugh Laing. It was a 54-year ordeal, too. When Tudor, on the greatest night of his life, received the Kennedy Center Honor, the troublesome Laing stayed home — in a sulk.

Lehman Engel must have been the busiest conductor on Broadway in the 1940s and '50s, that great age of the Broadway musical. Although he composed some fine incidental music for dozens of plays and wrote many lively books on the musical theatre, his true home was at the podium. *Li'l Abner, Wonderful Town, I Can Get It for You Wholesale,* and scores of other shows were first played for a grateful public by this charming little man. Hollywood engaged his services, too, and while there he became close to Montgomery Clift. What a shame that some of the energy churning through this tireless musician couldn't have been channeled into saving the doomed actor.

Snob *extraordinaire* and effortless charmer; languid layabout and industrious poet; Robert, Comte de Montesquiou, was the model, to the life, for Proust's perverse Baron de Charlus. And Proust wasn't the only one to dig nuggets from the count's life to create a literary character. Part of him found its way into Wilde's Dorian Gray and into Rostand's Peacock in Chanticleer. Montesquiou lived for beauty, a glutton for ornament, and could dismiss a friend pitilessly for not coming up to snuff. This man who was the personification of the sinuous curves of art nouveau affected to fall in love with various women, but the mauve-lined dandy in him won out every time.

Killer fruits. That was Truman Capote's memorable phrase to describe destructive, self-loathing homosexuals. Here, enjoying a thoroughly conjectural post-poke smoke, are two prime examples: Senator Joe McCarthy, scourge of the charcoal gray fifties, and his chief counsel, the repulsive Roy Cohn. Rumors of his homosexuality dogged McCarthy all through his brief, baleful career. The reptilian Cohn was different: *everybody* knew. Promiscuous but secretive, he was savage in his opposition to gay rights. And the cowardly shit died in the closet. Of AIDS. Oh, well, we can't *all* be graceful, tasteful, witty, and kind.

up. The ol' cowhand above, Aaron Copland, is probably the American composer who most effectively captures the authentic American sound. His orchestration is unmistakable, easily identifiable to even the tin-eared. For his themes he chose the homespun (the ballets *Billy the Kid* and *Rodeo*), the exalted (*Canticle of Freedom*), and sometimes a combination of the two (*Fanfare for the Common Man*). His talent spread out in all directions: film music, song cycles, symphonies and chamber music. He was married, and with children — like Leonard Bernstein, with whom he also shared another charming characteristic.

frica, especially in the nineteenth century, was a rich field for plunder by the nations of Europe, Britain most of all. Cecil Rhodes, the son of a clergyman, made a fortune in the Kimberley diamond fields, founded the de Beers Mining Company, and became virtual dictator of the southern end of Africa *and* prime minister of Cape Colony: a busy little bee by any measure. Although he reformed education, he also restricted voting to the literate, thereby effectively keeping power in white hands, a policy still in effect today. But he founded the Rhodes scholarships, and lovingly tended the country named Rhodesia in his honor. And, oh, yes — he was one of our own.

WILLHOITE

uick! How many black gay male science fiction writers can you name? And how many as good-looking as Samuel R. Delany? He was a prodigy, writing eight or nine novels in his early teens — though none were published. Still, not a bad start for a kid with dyslexia. At nineteen, he published one, *The Jewels of Aptor*, a paraphrase of the story of Jason's Argonauts, but also a full-blooded and original creation in itself. He grew more confident, more prolific, and he continues to do fine work. His best book, however, may not even be science fiction. *The Motion of Light in Water* is an intoxicating memoir of his early days in the East Village, when he first savored the great world, its fancies and fleshpots.

The byzantine sexual labyrinth of the Bloomsbury Group is probably more famous than the work they produced. Economist John Maynard Keynes, shown above, was the lover of painter Duncan Grant, who in turn was the lover of writer Lytton Strachey, who *then* ... well, never mind. It was all quite confusing. At any rate, Keynes, to the utter astonishment of the male Bloomsberries he'd been blithely boinking, fell in love with ballerina Lydia Lopokova. Such a *conventional* move scandalized his unconventional friends to their knickers, but it turned out to be a workable, loving marriage.

The Garbo movie got it all wrong. The real Queen Christina of Sweden looked more like a basset hound than a movie star. (Garbo, on the other hand, was no scholar.) Christina was determined to haul provincial Sweden kicking and screaming into the Age of Reason, and even lured Descartes north to complete the process. Her most enduring love was one of her ladies-in-waiting, Ebba Sparre. But Christina wearied of the monarchy. She slipped out of Sweden disguised as a man (a fake mustache and a pair of brogues might have been enough), converted to Catholicism at Innsbruck, and moved to Rome. A *successful* convert, all things considered — she's buried in St. Peter's.

dd family, the Bensons. The archbishop had three sons and a daughter, *all* gay. And when the good churchman shuffled off this mortal coil, his widow changed her name from Minnie to Ben. Hmmm. All three sons were very prolific authors. E.F. Benson, the best of the lot, was a volcano of words, belching out mysteries and ghost stories, reminiscences, and comic novels with a gay sensibility so thick you could spread it on a scone. All but forgotten for thirty years, his Lucia novels burst back into print in the 1970s, and many of his others followed. Poor man easily admitted he was gay, but probably never acted on it. A *gentleman*, you know.

Rudi Gernreich was the high-wire act of the 1960s fashion scene. A pioneer in the unisex look, he put *la différence* back on page one with his notorious topless bathing suit in 1964. Gernreich started out as a dancer. When the young Viennese emigrant landed here, Los Angeles beckoned. There he met Harry Hay, and together they founded the Mattachine Society, the first great vessel of Gay Liberation. Gernreich, after his fashion career blossomed, was something of a silent partner, never commenting on gay issues publicly. But after his death from lung cancer, his estate handsomely provided a trust to provide legal help and education for gay men and lesbians.

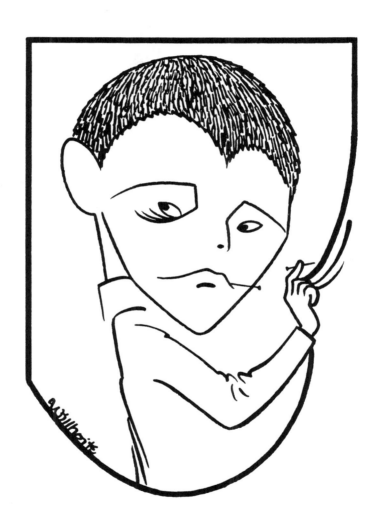

 ay Republicans? The gentleman from Connecticut, Stewart Brett McKinney, was one. He was born at the height of the Depression in hardscrabble Pennsylvania, which gave him some insight into people with troubles. He first wet his feet politically at age thirty-five, when he was elected to the Connecticut General Assembly. Re-elected easily, he served as minority leader, and on the side was director of the Bridgeport Hospital and worked for the local chamber of commerce as well. In 1971 he hit Washington, representative to the 92nd Congress. Though firmly pro-military, he was a good crusading liberal on civil rights issues. He was re-elected eight more times, till he succumbed to AIDS at the age of fifty-six.

igel Nicolson, in his memoir of his parents *Portrait of a Marriage,* spilled every last bean — which wouldn't have bothered either parent in the least. When Harold Nicolson married Vita Sackville-West, he probably intended to settle down to a perfectly conventional marriage. When his wife ran off to France with Violet Trefusis, it *did* rankle for a bit, but she returned and he accepted that she would never be the dutiful, straight wife. It didn't matter; he was gay anyway. A diplomat and writer who knew simply *everybody,* he published several fat volumes of diaries, letters, and reminiscences. She wrote novels and books on gardening. Each took lovers, and they all lived happily ever after.

hat in the world is *she* doing here? Anne Frank, a *lesbian?* Well, no, not strictly speaking, and unfortunately we'll never know how she would have developed. The facts are these: in her brave diary she could rhapsodize over the female body and wonder in perfect innocence what it would be like to make love to another girl. These details only came to light with the recent publication of the text of the entire (and previously censored) diary. Whether she did act or would have acted on these feelings is immaterial. The only thing of importance is the warm light shining from her great, inspiring, and imperishable spirit.

WILLHOITE

Glenway Wescott's output came in short, potent spurts (readers, contain yourselves!). His first book was poetry, *The Bitterns*, but he found the short novel to be his forte. His literary perspective was that of an expatriate midwesterner, but his very limited body of work hardly exploited it for all it was worth. He blossomed early at twenty-six with a superb novel, *The Grandmothers,* then lay fallow. But not alone: Monroe Wheeler was to become his lifelong lover. A second, late flowering produced two more short novels, *Apartment in Athens* and *The Pilgrim Hawk,* and he fell silent again. His final book was posthumous, a collection of diaries, *Continual Lessons.*

ackson Pollock would die of spontaneous combustion if he knew he were in this book! (And if he weren't dead already...) A brawling, woman-chasing stud who wore his pecker on his sleeve, he *could* be had by men; all it took was about a quart of whiskey. Yeah, one of those. In Pollock's early work, one can see the influences of Indian sand paintings, the great Mexican muralists, and even his early mentor, Thomas Hart Benton. The "action painting" that later made him a modern legend was the natural culmination of this lifetime of painting, but it was also a pretty good reflection of his slam-bang life. In those gigantic, turgid canvases we can see the man himself.

Powerful if inelegant prose: that was the judgment of early reviewers of the work of Djuna Barnes. That changed quickly. T.S. Eliot, no less, wrote in the introduction to her dark novel *Nightwood* of her "beauty of phrasing, the brilliance of wit and characterization, and a quality of horror and doom ... related to that of Elizabethan tragedy." Clearly, Barnes was not destined for the best-seller lists. By the time of her death, she was all but forgotten, but since then, her work has been reissued in a steady trickle. Particularly noteworthy is *The Ladies' Almanack,* a playful satire of Paris's expatriate lesbian community. From time to time, Barnes illustrated her own work, and in this *jeu d'esprit* it sparkles.

Empress of the Blues. That was Bessie Smith, a singer of absolutely no delicacy. Hell, she didn't need it. She had oceans of talent, confidence, and a pair of lungs that could send a song hurtling to the back of any house without amplification. A mean drunk and vicious street fighter, she was also a voracious lesbian who wasn't above devouring any *man* she took a fancy to. Listen to "Nobody Knows You When You're Down and Out" or "Empty Bed Blues." It's all there. Bessie died an ugly death, in Mississippi, hemorrhaging from an auto accident. Details vary, but most agree that the white hospitals turned her away. And an empress was allowed to die like a dog in the road.

Let the bullets that rip through my brain smash through every closet door in the nation." Harvey Milk knew he would become a gay martyr. The San Francisco City Hall killings of Milk and Mayor George Moscone on November 27, 1978, resonated throughout the nation like one of the city's famous quakes. When City Supervisor Dan White was convicted of manslaughter, not murder, rioting by furious lesbians and gay men broke out. Like Stonewall, like the 1992 Republican National Convention, such outrages fuel the movement. So Harvey Milk was right. For his full story, read Randy Shilts's excellent *The Mayor of Castro Street*.

ne of the more tempestuous barnstorming actresses of the nineteenth century was Adah Isaacs Menken, shown here in her most successful role, *Mazeppa.* Born in rather shady circumstances (four different fathers are cited in her own statements) in New Orleans, young Adah threw herself into the arts. Quadrilingual, versed in the classics, she could sing, dance, sculpt, paint, *and* write poetry. At twenty-two she hit the stage: the little dynamo had found her calling. In no time she was world-famous, the toast of New York, London, and Paris. In the time-honored tradition of actresses, she married repeatedly — four times in all — and made the time for a few women as well. Small wonder she was gathered to Abraham's bosom as a tender bud of thirty-three.

All hail the Nabob of Sob! Of all the pop singers of the fifties, Johnnie Ray had to be the oddest. Gawd! you had to be there to believe it, the hordes of screaming, weeping women. Of course his big hit was "Cry" (which spawned dozens of parodies), but it seems in retrospect that most of his hit songs were a shade lachrymose. He *can't* have been happy: almost totally deaf, unhappily married (a few short months after being arrested for — er, uh, falling in love with an undercover cop), messily divorced. Not even a *very* visible affair with Dorothy Kilgallen could disguise the fact that his heart was essentially given to his own sex. Why, it's enough to make a man cry...

Poor John Addington Symonds was determined to be unhappy. In his journals he poured forth detail upon detail of his relentless pursuit of sex — every stroke of it furtive, joyless, and guilt-ridden. In spite of this bizarre refusal to give over to pleasure, he wrote widely in support of the rights of "inverts." (Big-hearted, *yes*, but was that "inverts" crack necessary?) Symonds wasn't just a cheerless proselytizer for the cause, but also a poet, critic, and biographer of a couple of us (Michelangelo, Sir Philip Sidney). He wrote travel books too, exiled as he was to Italy, to escape the British damp — and the outraged fathers of a few boys.

Nobody should be surprised that Michel Foucault's *History of Sexuality* fills six volumes. The wonder is that it doesn't fill more than that. Foucault was not a philosopher but, rather, taught philosophy. He studied psychiatry, but found understanding of the psyche to be as illusory as philosophical certainty. So his life work became man's search for knowledge and truth. After all, the journey, not the arrival, matters. Among such weighty tomes as *The Archeology of Knowledge* and *Madness and Civilization*, he did manage to produce a charming little study on Magritte. Obviously a dour type, he must certainly have had time for a *little* fun.

etween various jobs ranging from waiter to longshoreman to male model, Claude McKay somehow managed to eke out a living as a writer. His poetry and novels (*Home to Harlem, Banjo,* etc.) secured his position as an eminence of the Harlem Renaissance. Jamaica-born, he traveled restlessly, first to Harlem, then Britain (where he was fêted and sponsored by George Bernard Shaw and Frank Harris), then France, Spain, and Morocco. *And* Russia, where, as a devoted leftist, he was lionized. Lost in the shuffle was a wife and child (marriage really wasn't his particular tango), and his life burnt out early. Just as well. He missed the witch-hunts of the fifties. As a *black* Communist, he wouldn't have had a prayer.

Madame Helena Rubinstein entered medical school in her hometown, Cracow, Poland. She rather liked laboratory work, but found that she didn't care much for *sick* people. What to do ... what to do...? Why, quit school, move to Australia, and make face cream, of course! The Australian women, eager to rise above the country's convict-colony origins, looked to Madame to give them polish. And she did. She opened the country's first beauty salon, made a bundle, and eventually developed over six hundred different beauty products. The rest of the world took note. Not even her arch-foe Elizabeth Arden could match her eventual haul: seven homes, multimillion-dollar collections of art and jewelry, and her own art museum in Tel Aviv.

Brian Epstein has gotten a lot of bad, homophobic press. Of course he was gay. Of course he loved John Lennon — he loved them all. And no wonder. He plucked the Fab Four out of a grungy rock-and-roll cellar in Liverpool and presented them to the world. They might very well have shot to stardom on their own, but everyone agrees he managed them brilliantly. But unrequited love is a mean master; add drugs, alcohol, and the poison of gay self-hatred, and you have a lethal mix. Poor Epstein tried girls (the mad animal pounce), but with no real success. And it all ended with an overdose.

 traight America is usually astonished when an athlete turns out to be gay, but, hey, all that grab-assing in the shower has to mean *something*, right? Glenn Burke, shown above, was expected to be "the next Willie Mays" — even if the (over-whelmingly) white managers always say that about any new black rookie. Burke started out in the Dodgers, in 1976. But the rumors and innuendo soon sent him *out* the window, traded to the Oakland A's. Two years later, he took the short trip across the bay: to San Francisco, leaving professional baseball forever.

othing is so effective for getting ahead as nepotism. Caius Julius Caesar Octavianus, a *pretty* child, knew that well. His great-uncle Julius Caesar, as a result, made him his heir. While young Caius was tooling around Illyrium, Caesar was assassinated, and the dutiful boy hightailed it back to Rome with revenge on his mind. Finally emperor, and rechristened Augustus Caesar (an honor conferred by the Senate), he made Rome glitter. Her roads were improved and her face was lifted. The emperor had no court, but declared himself merely the first citizen of Rome. He was a great patron of the arts, and was succeeded by his stepson Tiberius, a *pretty* child...

Vienna has musicians like Venice has pigeons. Schubert, Mozart, Brahms, Beethoven, all manner of Strausses — you name 'em. And one of the flowers of the American musical theatre springs from the same soil, too: Frederick Loewe. With the almost egregiously straight Alan Jay Lerner, he created one brilliant musical after another. *The Day before Spring. Paint Your Wagon.* When they played music from a work-in-progress for Mary Martin, she wailed to her husband afterward: "Oh, those dear boys have lost their talent!" But the rest of Broadway — and the world — thought better of *My Fair Lady.* Then came *Gigi,* a perfect film musical. Then *Camelot.* I guess Mary Martin was wrong...

creaming popes, mutilation, naked male bodies smeared across the canvas — Francis Bacon's paintings *are* alarming. Their horror, despair, and, strangely, their voluptuousness are meant to comment on the brutality of the twentieth century, and they do — effectively. The artist himself looked like something begotten by an owl upon a particularly peevish flounder, malign, squat, and sullen. But, no, Bacon was gentle, urbane, witty, and fond of good food and wine. The son of a horsetrainer, he was kicked out of his home for shtupping the grooms in the barn, but it never bothered him. ("Being homosexual I have lived with the most marvelously disastrous people.") His painting grew in power and rage, and he died happy and honored.

he late Australian entertainer and songwriter Peter Allen was something to see on stage, a one-man fireworks display. He pounded the piano, leaped about like a stag in heat, and sang with the fervor of a wolf baying at the moon. Not one of your more restful types. And although gay, he married a woman with an energy level roughly comparable to his own: Liza Minnelli. Not one of your more restful marriages, either. Oh well, at least it was brief. Peter would play with — and to — the audiences' expectations, announcing, "Yes — what you've heard is true! I am — Australian!" His last years were unhappy: *Legs Diamond*, the Broadway musical he wrote and starred in, flopped resoundingly. He could take *anything* but rejection.

omaine Brooks wasn't a terribly good painter, but given her upbringing, it was remarkable that she achieved anything at all. Brooks was the product of a simply horrible home life, a gothic hell created by one of the all-time great monster mothers. Ella Goddard apotheosized her son, a pathetic wretch who dwindled into madness, and maltreated her daughter dementedly. To save herself, Brooks fled to Paris to paint. A brief marriage to homosexual poet John Ellingham Brooks and a torrid affair with straight poet Gabriele D'Annunzio had to be gotten out of the way before she found her true love, Natalie Clifford Barney.

f the fecund literary triumvirate of the 1930s, Auden, Isherwood, and Stephen Spender, only the last remains. Tall, hawkish, and elegantly lean in his youth, he is still the same, but with a coronet of white hair rising above. He made his reputation as a poet, one of the so-called Oxford Group, as political as they were poetical. He even joined the Communist Party briefly in 1936–1937, but left in disillusion; the intellectual path that led him to remove himself from the party is explained eloquently in his book *The God That Failed.* In his later years, poetry has bowed aside for prose. Married with grandchildren, he was somewhat more, er, *unbuttoned* in his impetuous youth.

Was Isadora Duncan a great artist or merely a poseur? A pioneer of the dance or a purveyor of poppycock? Since early twentieth-century dance is more or less written on the wind or at best pinned to a few faded photographs, we have only the testimony of her contemporaries. However she is judged, she changed the face of dance forever. Duncan was bedded by a number of noteworthy men, but like most free spirits she was pansexual. Alas, her colorful death has almost overshadowed her life. Riding in an open car, her long scarf caught in the spokes of the wheel and garotted her. We don't have more than a few scraps of film of Duncan dancing, but what we do have may be even better: Vanessa Redgrave, in the movie *The Loves of Isadora,* gives one of the greatest performances ever put on celluloid.

Until Dame Edna Everage hit these shores, female impersonation was a minority pleasure, limited largely to gay clubs and the occasional Rotary Club show. One man made it pretty far into the center ring, though: the late T.C. Jones. A decade of chorus work in New York; the Provincetown Playhouse (where he first found his *métier*, drag); then nightclubs, where he was spotted by Leonard Sillman. The producer put T.C. into *New Faces of 1956*. Finally, he was made. He even hit "The Ed Sullivan Show" — three times! — and one memorably macabre installment of "Alfred Hitchcock Presents."

ho among us couldn't make a fool of himself over a beautiful but dumb boy? Hell, who *hasn't?* King Louis XIII of France certainly did, with one of his pages. And as beautiful but dumb boys will, the page eventually done him wrong. Some men never learn. The poor king was a gentle queen, melancholy by nature, and was content to let Cardinal Richelieu do all the dirty work of his reign. The Marquis de Cinq-Mars became the king's lover, and some say that the Machiavellian cardinal steered the dashing nobleman into the queen's chamber. If that's true, it's likely that Louis XIV, the Sun King, was not necessarily the son-king ... Hmmm ... rather a tangled situation.

Contentious and erudite, Gore Vidal displays a mandarin writing style, a true sense of history, and a firm grasp of American politics. This gives him equal stature in criticism and fiction — and didn't exactly hurt him in his portrayal of a professional politician in the film *Bob Roberts*. He's a particularly protean man of letters: the scabrous satirist (*Myra Breckinridge*) slips easily into the province of the Serious Historical Novelist (*Burr, Lincoln*). Vidal is a brilliant critic and essayist, and a playwright, too. (Though he must have gasped with horror when told that his play *Visit to a Small Planet* was to be filmed as a vehicle for Jerry Lewis.) And what a dinner companion he must be!

ho's the swiniest swine in the world? Why, Captain Hook, of course! As portrayed once and for all time by the great Cyril Ritchard. He was completely a man of the theatre, appearing in only four films, including *Blackmail*, one of Alfred Hitchcock's silent films, as — improbably — a would-be rapist. Though the Australian actor and director was long married to actress Madge Elliott, he was *rather* a closet case. "I do wish that years ago," wrote Noel Coward, a pretty unimpeachable source, "that Cyril had faced up to the fact that he's as queer as a coot."

WILLHOITE

Greek-American conductor Dmitri Mitropoulos died, during a rehearsal, with the strains of Mahler's Third echoing in his ears. Some echo — some *ears.* He was born in Athens, the son of a leather merchant. A child prodigy at the piano, he eventually became a student of gay composer Ferruccio Busoni. In Berlin, his conducting was noticed, and the great turning point in his career came when he substituted for ailing pianist Egon Petri, conducting from the keyboard — and from memory — Prokofiev's Third Piano Concerto. Even Prokofiev declared that he could never have done it himself. Mitropolous never married — with all that implies.

61

In Victoria's glorious reign, the British lion roamed the globe, bringing Civilization, Commerce, and Christianity to the teeming heathen masses. And if these imperial adventures resulted in a little bloodshed, that's the way the crumpet crumbles. After all, Florence Nightingale could clean up the mess. Nursing incarnate, the angel of the battlefield, she was a dynamo, consumed by the flame of Duty. In short, a monomaniac worthy of being irreverently enshrined by Strachey in his *Eminent Victorians*. In the Crimean War, she defined what nursing should be: total care, at any hour. Hence the appellation the Lady with the Lamp. As she slept with duchesses and chambermaids, the lamp *must* have come in handy.

Playwright Lillian Hellman was well known as the lover of crime novelist Dashiell Hammett, but also had a number of liaisons with other women. When her writing for the theatre began to dry up, she smoothly changed gears and became a distinguished memoirist. *Pentimento* and *An Unfinished Woman* are superb. An odor of sanctity and self-congratulation, however, creeps into *Scoundrel Time*, an account of her admittedly gutsy stand against McCarthyism. She was less lucky in her tangle with another McCarthy — Mary, who publicly called Hellman a pathological liar. Hellman sued for slander, but died before the case came to trial. She was a fighter, all right. Looked like one, too.

ere's another fine writer who fell afoul of the ferocious Mary McCarthy. When Doris Grumbach wrote *The Company She Kept*, her study of the writer, McCarthy swooped down on her like the wolf on the fold, howling lawsuit. The suit was withdrawn, the book limped into print shorn of some of its goodies, and Grumbach returned triumphantly to fiction, with *Chamber Music.* A few whiners tut-tutted over the lesbian affair of Caroline and Anna, but generally it got raves. Teacher, editor, and bookstore owner, Grumbach was the sage of Washington, D.C., until the savagery of the city drove her — and companion Sybil — to rural Maine.

Franz Schubert wasn't always the pudgy little person we see above. In his salad days he was quite a dish. In fact, he started out as a choirboy — and we all know what *they're* like ... His role as an interpreter of music changed as his voice did; at the keyboard, he presided over the Schubertiads, Viennese musicales to which everyone panted for admittance. As a symphonist, Schubert could hold his head high in the company of Brahms or Beethoven. His chamber music is enchanting. And he wrote a body of over eight hundred brilliant songs, every one a gem, and some, like *An Silvia*, diamond-perfect.

ot much is expected of the sons of the rich, especially those who choose to, well, *dabble* in the arts. The case of Francis Poulenc was no different — at first. But if a caterpillar can become a butterfly, a dilettante can metamorphose into a composer of grace and power. Even Stravinsky, a radically different kind of composer, admired his work. Poulenc's music for piano and orchestra, especially, is the essence of French insouciance shot through with deeper feelings. His opera *Dialogues of the Carmelites* — the last scene in particular — can raise the hair on the back of the neck. His longtime lover was baritone Pierre Bernac, for whom he wrote some gorgeous songs.

Regular readers of the *New York Times* know that Craig Claiborne is *the* final arbiter on matters gustatorial. A sometime restaurant reviewer, his greater fame is as the author of a whole flotilla of cookbooks, alone or in collaboration with French chef Pierre Franay. The flagship is, of course, *The New York Times Cookbook.* Though the toast of Manhattan, he's still a southern boy at heart. In his memoir *A Feast Made for Laughter*, he writes warmly of his ties to the South. Always frank about his homosexuality, he is even franker about his incestuous relationship with his doomed, unhappy father.

Heldentenor. No, that's not a tenor who sings like hell, but it's probably not a bad working definition, either. Lauritz Melchior, the greatest "heroic tenor" of the century in the opinion of many, was Danish (which must have chagrined the Wagner-worshipping Nazis). Not only was his voice powerful, supple, and beautiful, he was considered an exciting actor as well. On the opera stage, that is. In Hollywood films, he was generally relegated to fatuous secondary roles. Still, he was the darling of the Met, and that was what counted most. He was also the darling, for a time, of the novelist Hugh Walpole.

reat Emancipators don't always wear beards. Susan B. Anthony would not rest until women had the vote, even though she was in her grave a decade before it was accomplished. And probably spinning. Anthony was a machine, a force, with an awesome singleness of purpose, and the ability to organize and galvanize others. But her human side is revealed in loving letters to Anna Dickinson. Virgil Thomson and Gertrude Stein (two more members of our tribe) collaborated on an opera with her as subject, *The Mother of Us All.* And to the American woman, she *was,* by God.

he elegant short stories of Hector Hugh Munro were written under the byline of Omar Khayyam's cupbearer: Saki. A taste for these deliciously poisonous bon-bons is said to be a specialized one — but most people share it. Witty, pungent, and utterly heartless, they have been steadily popular since their first appearance in 1904. Munro was born in Burma, and reared in Devonshire, unhappy and sensitive, contemptuous of the conventional. In essence, he *was* Conradin, the boy in his story "Sredni Vashtar" — though presumably without a satanic ferret at his summons. Munro enlisted when the Great War broke out, stepped on a German mine, and Jesus had him for a sunbeam.

When you're scrawny and funny-looking, the great romantic ballet roles tend to elude one's grasp. But with talent and balls and stick-to-it-iveness, you can get by. Sir Robert Helpmann danced more great character roles than most other first-rate dancers. (A standout was one of the ugly stepsisters in Cinderella, with Sir Frederick Ashton playing the other.) A protean little wisp, Helpmann was also a fine choreographer, a revue artist, and a Shakespearean actor. He even played Hamlet at Stratford-on-Avon, but was perhaps more at home at the Old Vic — playing opposite Vivien Leigh — as Oberon, King of the Fairies (*no* jokes, please) in *A Midsummer Night's Dream.*

Libby Holman was celebrated as a blues singer — but not for the trueness of her notes, which tended to wobble alarmingly. Listen to her version of "Love for Sale." Part of the fascination is waiting breathlessly to see if she will run off the rails entirely. She did have a good steady vibrato, though. But, what the hell, she was less famous for her singing than for her tendency to bury husbands. She was even charged with the murder of one, the young scion of the R.J. Reynolds Tobacco Company. (Her luck with women was better.) The Reynolds family pulled strings, and she was never tried, but the scandal pretty well did her career in. In the fifties she attempted a halfhearted comeback on Broadway in a one-woman show, *Blues, Ballads and Sin-Songs.*

The rumors of George Gershwin's homosexuality still swirl, though there's hardly a whiff of it in his reverential biographies. America's most popular and highly regarded composer was essentially a tunesmith; his music was all orchestrated by others. But what a tunesmith! *Porgy and Bess* is without question the great American opera. His orchestral works actually grow in popularity every year. But his finest work is probably the incredible body of theatre and film songs he wrote with his equally gifted brother Ira — lovely little miracles of collaboration. Still, one wonders what George felt setting to music the lyric from *Girl Crazy:* "...on western prairies we shoot the fairies or send them back to the east."

James Beard, the gargantuan gastronome above, was a gustatory adventurer before he was a year old: he consumed, by himself, a huge onion, skin and all. His mother, with her Chinese cook and a formidable knowledge of international cuisine, ran her kitchen like that of a restaurant. Jimmy, underfoot, absorbed everything she knew, so he became a chef. In his twenty-three cookbooks, he avoided all the jargon that made American cooks so fearful of gourmet cuisine. With Julia Child, he demystified it, and thereby changed the way America eats. A gay extrovert, he was nonetheless deeply closeted. It must have been a pretty fair-sized walk-in.

This saturnine individual is Henri III, King of France, and he might very well have married Elizabeth the Great of England. He declined, he said, on religious grounds, but one must take into account his mignons. These were, according to the *Encyclopedia Britannica*, "a small group of handsome young men with whom he indulged in questionable excesses." Henri was a pretty mixed bag: an intellectual with cultivated tastes, but a ruthless man who, before ascending the French throne, instigated the St. Bartholomew's Day Massacre. It was a rocky reign, too, and when he died, the last of the Valois line (one need hardly wonder why...), France was in the toils of civil war.

illie Jean King's star has fallen slightly, as an athlete's eventually must, but in the seventies she was a dazzler. She scored a big one for women everywhere when she skunked the porker Bobby Riggs on the tennis court, but couldn't quite pull her dignity together later when she was sued for palimony by a lover. Martina Navratilova, on the other hand...! Czechoslovakia's loss is our gain. She's still the greatest tennis player alive, and has more class than any ten male players (who tend to be a childish, blustery lot anyway). She's open, out, and as tireless a worker for gay and lesbian causes as she is brilliant on the court.

egional writer: that's a hard label to shake, and all through his distinguished career, William Goyen tried hard to do so. In Texas he is venerated; beyond the borders of the state his work is merely respected. Still, his 1950 novel *The House of Breath* will always have its readers. It's virtually plotless fantasia (clearly influenced by Thomas Wolfe) of a house, a river, and the town of Charity, Texas. The lyrical quality in this book was to be found in all his subsequent novels and stories, not to mention the plays he adapted from his own work. Though bisexual he was married to the character actress Doris Roberts.

Brendan Behan was not a prolific writer — but what he managed to belch forth has the authentic stink of genius. He didn't have the time to write much, what with boozing and brawling. It appears he was trying to out-Dylan Dylan Thomas and the results were similar: a small body of simply terrific work, a liver turned to tapioca, and an early death. *The Quare Fellow* and (especially) *The Hostage* show how brilliantly he could bring life to the stage. (The drag queen Rio Rita in the latter is especially flavorful.) Revolutionary activities for the I.R.A. sent him to prison for three years in the early forties, resulting in his book *Borstal Boy*, a bawdy, exquisitely obscene depiction of prison life, with *ALL* its ... er, fun activities.

I t fell to a young English girl, Eva Le Gallienne, to provide the American stage with the paradigm of a great classical actress. She made her stage debut in London in 1914, and soon set sail for New York. "Too English," she finally got parts by coaching the English roses out of her voice. Her first play here was short-lived, which gave her time to read — and she discovered Ibsen. She was his vociferous champion (here she appears as Mrs. Alving in *Ghosts*) but also played Shakespeare and contemporary playwrights with easy facility. With her lover Marion Evensen, she settled in Connecticut, but made three forays into Hollywood, and she died at ninety-two, honored and loved and with seventy-seven years of show business under her belt.

ete Townshend, of the Who, recently revealed his bisexuality; it can't have come as a shock to anyone who listened carefully to some of the lyrics he wrote in the group's early days. England was pretty blasé about rock lyrics featuring masturbation and general genderfuck, but American radio station owners got downright edgy. The Who were a great group, but they really scaled Parnassus in 1969, with *Tommy*, the first rock opera. It took *twenty-four* years to get it to Broadway. On wax, an outlay of $36,000 did it; the stage show gobbled up six million. Hey, things change. The old guitar-smasher himself is clean, sober, and sheared all-but-bald. But not mellow. Not yet.

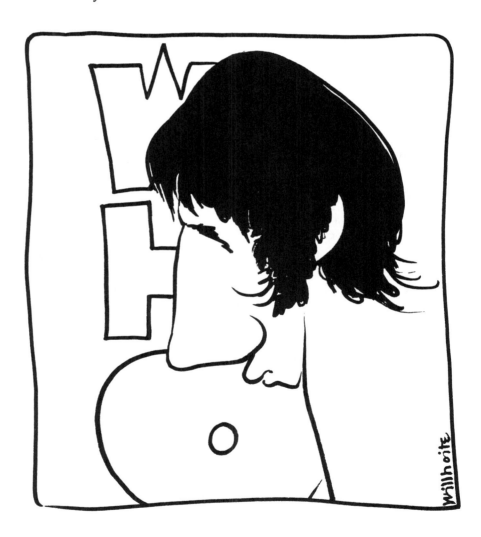

enaissance Man, in our pedestrian age, is a term carelessly applied to any poor putz who can balance a checkbook, strum a guitar on weekends, and maybe write a letter without disgracing himself. In Good Queen Bess's Golden Days the term was more hard-won, and its finest embodiment was Sir Philip Sidney. A courtier to the queen, he was groomed equally for statesmanship and for the field of valor. As poet he wrote *Astrophel and Stella*, the finest of Elizabethan sonnet sequences — and love poems to Fulke Greville, Lord Brooke. When he died at the Battle of Zutphen of a shattered thigh, he was only thirty-two, and was buried in St. Paul's to the lamentation of a grateful nation.

he gentleman shown above is George Kelly. He was Grace's uncle — yes, *that* Grace Kelly. In his time, though, he was known for more than his family connections. In the 1920s, '30s, and '40s his plays commanded the New York stage. *Craig's Wife* was filmed twice, with Joan Crawford and Rosalind Russell — and even won the Pulitzer Prize. Other plays like *Behold the Bridegroom* and *The Fatal Weakness* were vastly popular too. *The Show-Off* was revived in the '70s as one of Helen Hayes's "farewell" performances. But today, Kelly's work is all but forgotten.

Scott Fitzgerald wrote: "There are no second acts in American lives." *Wrong.* Many blues aficionados think of Alberta Hunter as a dignified, silken old lady who suddenly broke onto the music scene in the 1980s. No, she was a sensation in the earlier decades, too, light, bright, one of the true queens of swing. Her upbeat rendition of "Miss Otis Regrets" is still the best one on records; she plays Cole Porter's satire right on the surface. But in the fifties she quit the music business and became a nurse. Later, when she was forcibly retired, back she came. And a star was reborn.

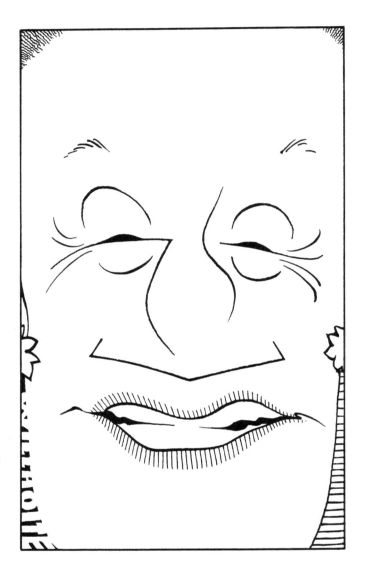

he most fabulously successful gay play was *The Boys in the Band,* by Mart Crowley. And never has a play dated so quickly, so utterly, so abysmally. True, the dialogue glitters. And it's catnip for actors. But gay self-hatred pervades the play like a champagne hangover. It was first produced in 1968. Next year came Stonewall — and the play was obsolete. What kept the play going, of course, was its discovery by straights; every stereotype they held dear was reinforced by the self-lacerating queens strutting and fretting on the stage. Crowley weighed in with another play, *A Breeze from the Gulf,* but it died, and his career as a playwright with it.

here he stands in a Boston park, a pedestal for pigeons. Not one in a thousand who passes the statue of Senator David Ignatius Walsh knows or remembers the scandal. But in 1942 the Massachusetts senator was chairman of the Senate Naval Affairs Committee. Near the Brooklyn Navy Yard one night, a "male brothel" was raided. The good senator had the good luck not to be there that night, but the bad luck to be cited as a regular by the owner. Ah, well. The tabloids had a field day, some bluenoses got to cluck disapprovingly, and a few sailors had the tar scared out of them. And Walsh? The Senate cleared him. And so he gets to preside over the park, the pigeons, and the pickups.

Central Casting could not have provided a more convincing tart spinster than Edna Ferber. Combative, opinionated, with a keen wit that could all but disembowel an opponent, she was also cherished for her generosity and warmth. That wit made her a charter member of the Algonquin Round Table, in the days when she collaborated with George S. Kaufman on exquisitely funny plays like *Dinner at Eight*. She became even more famous for her big, outdoorsy novels like *So Big* and *Cimarron*. Obsessive about her privacy, she wrote two guarded books of memoirs, but after her death it fell to her great-niece to write of Edna's lesbianism.

ou are a born critic and you will be a distinguished one," said Van Wyck Brooks of Newton Arvin — when Arvin was a mere tot of twenty-two. The young man went on to write critical essays in the *New Republic* and the *Nation,* and perceptive studies of Whitman, Hawthorne, and, most insightfully, Melville. He was an early mentor of gay writers Truman Capote and Carson McCullers, and flirted with communism, which gave him a few uncomfortable moments during the 1950s political inquisition. Worse was to come: in 1960, he and two other Smith College professors were arrested for "homosexual lewdness." His conviction, suspended sentence, and fine broke him, and this witty, shy, and learned man died two years later.

ost theologians, I imagine, are not into wife-swapping. Paul Tillich, however, was a pioneer in sexual experimentation of all kinds: "Dionysian proclivity," as the sober *Dictionary of American Biography* delightfully puts it. Boys, girls, possibly penguins ... who knows? Serving in the German Army during World War I, Tillich was permanently altered by the gut-wrenching horror. His idealistic program was abandoned, and the structure of society got a harder, longer look. The Nazis were a little less than wild about him (Jewish friends, you know), so he packed up and came to America. His lectures and sermons, directed largely at the religiously disaffected, earned him the sobriquet "Apostle of the Skeptics."

In the company of her pal Picasso, Marie Laurencin is only a minor painter — let's say in the middle ranks of the second-rate. Her subject matter was domestic to a fault: mothers, babies, and young girls, painted in flat pretty pastels, without the transforming talent of, say, a Mary Cassatt. Her milieu was Paris in the time of great, tumultuous artistic ferment, and if she only skirted the major movements, she was at least prolific. And versatile: she made prints, illustrated books, and designed sets for the stage. Once the mistress of the poet Guillaume Apollinaire, she eventually found Suzanne Morand — and happiness.

dward VIII of England was a romantic popinjay as a prince, and a total washout as a king; only as the Duke of Windsor did he find his true niche. Still, there was always something a bit unhealthy about the Duke and his Duchess. He seemed a satellite to her, this virago with a mouth like a paper cut and the cool appraising eyes of an auctioneer. They glided serenely through life accepting tribute, ornaments to society — and of no earthly use to anybody. All his life, the Duke was assumed to be gay, and as a result was a vicious, knee-jerk homophobe.

Willhoite

Concerning the Eccentricities of Cardinal Pirelli. Valmouth. Vainglory. The Flower Beneath the Foot. These books, darlings, are the exquisite fruit borne by the oh-so-very late Ronald Firbank, violet-scented English novelist. Ah, lapidary! fragrant! — and of a preciosity which would make the Divine Oscar himself seem a hairy-armed barbarian. Ooooooooh! Peopled by a host of randy clergymen, royalty, and society butterflies with wicked tongues, his novels are being rediscovered on a small scale. The witty dialogue, improbable situations, and outlandish elegance in his work are utterly unique.

Frederick Rolfe, self-styled Baron Corvo, was a failed priest, a drunk, a druggie, a thief, an ingrate to his publishers — and a one-of-a-kind writer. He was also the apotheosis of the English eccentric and ended his days as a babbling wraith haunting the canals of Venice. Of all his crabbed, Byzantine books, the most representative — and the closest to his own life — was *Hadrian the Seventh*, a wish-fulfillment fantasia about — yes — a failed priest who by a series of flukes becomes pope. The pathetic hero was the closest Rolfe ever came to a confession. But anyone wanting the real scoop should read *The Quest for Corvo* by A.J.A. Symons, itself as hypnotic, as improbable as its subject.

Popes. Saintly types, right? Busy with good works and devotion to the flock and almsgiving and prayer from dawn to bedtime, right? Well, not always. During the Middle Ages, the papacy was more or less up for grabs, and quite a few popes were just downright BAD. One of the worst of a bad lot was Benedict IX, who was bumped onto the throne of St. Peter at the advanced age of twelve. God's work definitely took a back seat to numerous sins of the flesh, particularly homosexual orgies. All the seven deadlies got a good workout, in fact, avarice especially: Benedict sold every office he could, even, finally, the papacy itself.

Sergei Eisenstein, with D.W. Griffith, created the screen vocabulary. Eisenstein's early film *Potemkin* established montage as a powerful tool for storytelling, and soon Russia's leadership knew they had *another* powerful tool in Eisenstein. Apart from their value as propaganda, his movies were given their due as art all over the world. Even Hollywood beckoned. How strange the Russian giant must have seemed there, a colossus striding beneath the palms. Any dreams of film-making in Hollywood soon died and he returned to the USSR to make *Ivan the Terrible.* But the second film of the trilogy incurred, somehow, the wrath of Stalin. The third was never made.

hen the late Charles Ludlam played a pugnacious little southern lawyer in the film *The Big Easy,* it must have been an exotic sight to his fans: he played it in suit and tie. The guiding spirit and diva-in-chief of the Ridiculous Theatrical Company, he was the most flamboyant of crossdressers, the Duse of Drag (best tip: fill your bra with birdseed). Nobody seeing him in the costume of Marguerite Gautier can ever watch *La Traviata* again without snickering. He wrote plays with delectable titles: *Turds in Hell, When Queens Collide, Eunuchs of the Forbidden City* — twenty-nine in all. His most famous is *The Mystery of Irma Vep,* now one of the most-produced plays in America.

ome time around 1890, in San Francisco, a chubby little girl was not invited to a posh kiddie party. In that early snub, thought Elsa Maxwell, was the genesis of her career as a legendary party-giver. But before she wriggled into the graces of Those Who Mattered, she toured in a Shakespeare company and played piano in honky-tonks. Part jereboam of champagne, part Little Brown Jug, Elsa was the great catalyst, whose talent lay in introducing people — and writing about it. For fifty years she was a tight buddy with fellow-gay Cole Porter (who worked her name into several lyrics), but, hell, *she knew everybody.*

ay Nazis? Yes, even the chief organizer of Hitler's *Sturmabteilung* (storm troopers) concealed a bit of lavender beneath his brown shirt. Poor Ernst Roehm! I guess if the face in your shaving mirror looks like a plum pudding nursing a secret sorrow, you *compensate.* And compensate he did. Early on he founded the National Socialist German Workers' Party — before Hitler. They were great pals, in fact, till Hitler realized this guy was perhaps *too* good an organizer ... So the blood purge of the S.A. was inevitable. Roehm and several of his gay companions were routed from their love nests one night and slaughtered on the orders of the Fuhrer — *the bitch!*

ccording to Suetonius, only one of the twelve Caesars, Claudius, kept strictly to women as bed partners. Perhaps the most fickle sexual opportunist of the lot was Julius Caesar, "a woman to every man, a man to every woman." Statesman, conqueror, man of letters, he's accounted the most eminent man of his age. But Caesar has always had his detractors. Was he a demagogue or a defender of liberty? His contemporaries could make no easy judgments. The orator Cicero, for instance, declared he would rather spend an evening in conversation with Caesar than in any other way. And Cicero hated him.

Poetry's loss was photography's inestimable gain. Minor White returned to his early love in 1937, spending his first productive years as a photographer for the Work Projects Administration, the results being more creative than documentary. In 1945 he studied with Edward Weston, which intensified the tonal beauty of his work; then with Alfred Steiglitz and Ansel Adams. But in style, White's work owed nothing to anyone, and the poet was set free in an altogether different medium. His nature studies are lovingly observed abstractions. But to the male nude he brought a lyrical passion, an eroticism unmatched until...

Art hath an enemy
called Ignorance.
—Ben Jonson

 obert Mapplethorpe. Everybody in our tribe knows his name by this time. When the Corcoran Gallery cravenly weaseled out of exhibiting the late photographer's work, a CAUSE was born. The time was the benighted Reagan years (don't get me started), and the howls of horror shook the National Endowment for the Arts to its shoes. Great press, though. What really matters is the work, which even apart from its sensational aspects is, well, *sensational*. Mapplethorpe's enormous flowers are as sexually saturated as his luscious male nudes — which are no more sensuous in turn than his portraits. Everything he shot pulsates with light and life.

Massachusetts's 10th District has sent Congressman Gerry Studds back to Washington every election year since 1972. Things were a trifle iffy for a while, though: in 1983 he was censured by the House for sexual misconduct. Now, members of Congress are as fond of hiding the salami as the rest of us, but this was slightly different: Studds had an affair with a seventeen-year-old male page. The media, of course, had a feast with the story, and the congressman was stripped of a subcommittee chairmanship. But he retained his seat. His largely blue-collar constituency has continued to see past his sexual preference, because he always keeps their interests at heart. There's something special about that Studds service.

A braggart who claimed to have discovered the source of the Nile (he hadn't) and to have been the first white man in Tibet (he wasn't), John Hanning Speke was a loner, an anti-intellectual, and a blithering neurotic. He attached himself to the great explorer Sir Richard Burton with an obsession that has been explained by some as desire. But the love turned into a towering hatred, and till his death he was Burton's nemesis. His fellow explorers were edgy about his refusal to touch women, disturbed by the savagery with which he killed animals (not sporting, you know, to kill *thousands*), and aghast at his penchant for eating the fetuses of his prey. Let's hope he at least *cooked* them first.

izzie Borden took an axe and gave her father forty whacks; when she saw what she had done, she gave her mother forty-one." The verses didn't get it quite right. It was a hatchet — a much more easily deployed weapon. And there were fewer blows, but enough to make mincemeat of Andrew Borden and his wife Abby, Lizzie's hated stepmother. Well, the sweet, virginal Sunday school teacher was acquitted, but the children of the neighborhood were wiser than the jury. Their taunting verses became part of our folklore. So Lizzie packed up and left town, as the lover of Nance O'Neal, a leading actress of the day.

Unless you're willing to provoke a nasty war with Norway or Finland, what's a modern king of Sweden to do? Well, if you're Gustav V, you play tennis. Gustav reigned longer than any other Swedish monarch, from 1907 to 1950, and he must have been monumentally bored. Although he dutifully performed his dynastic duties, by marrying Victoria of Baden and siring a new king, he was probably more concerned with working on the old backhand, or cozying up to a page or two. He really was quite dull, I suppose, but in twentieth-century Sweden, that's probably just what was required. His people loved him, for his fuzzy balls perhaps, or, more likely, for the model he set for neutrality in the World Wars.

Stalin's Englishmen were a complicated lot. These two, Guy Burgess (top) and Donald Maclean (bottom) will be forever bracketed, even if their sexual liaison is, shall we say, academic. Both were gay, and calamitously alcoholic. In Cambridge, where they met, they espoused communism, but each was too great a snob to truly embrace The Worker — except as rough trade, for which each had a *marked* taste. Poor boys — they weren't happy even when they had to flee to Russia. Guy lost half his teeth in a beating, and was denied all privileges by the government. And poor Donald, who had finally convinced himself he was straight, lost his wife to the slimily charming Kim Philby. It's difficult to care.

hey called him Big Bill. And he was. William Tatem Tilden, Jr., stood tall among the colorful figures of the 1920s. One of America's greatest tennis players, he won seven U.S. Championships, three Wimbledons, two professional titles, and was instrumental in keeping the Davis Cup in America for seven straight years, from 1920 to 1926. Tall and imposing as a stag, he had a powerful serve and was perfectly willing to show a bit of temperament. Everybody loved Big Bill. He was *especially* popular with the law, who arrested him a couple of times for having sex with adolescent boys.

ergei Pavlovich Diaghilev did more for the ballet than anyone else in the first half of the twentieth century. But at what cost! The impresario of the Ballets Russes was nurturer and destroyer at the same time. He was indispensable to the careers of composers Stravinsky, Debussy, Ravel, and Milhaud; to choreographers Fokine, Balanchine, Lifar, and Massine; and to numberless dancers, prominent among them Pavlova, Markova, Dolin, and Nijinsky. His alliance with the latter, however, was a *disaster*. Both employer and devilishly possessive lover, he kept poor Nijinsky jumping like a puppet, withdrawing and reinstating both love and professional support in a dizzying cycle.

Edith Piaf — the Little Sparrow — began life as Edith Giovanna Gassion. Life was hard from an early age, but she was able to turn her travail into an art that made her an idol to millions. At fifteen she was singing for centimes in the street, then cafes, then cabarets — the toast of Paris, then all of Europe, then America. All this sounds like cheap fiction, but it was all true, and perfectly lovely. She even made a handful of movies; one, *Le Bel Indifférent,* was originally a play written for her by Cocteau. The power of her waiflike appeal was a passport to the beds of many men and even a few women, notably Marlene Dietrich — who got around...

109

O h, there's something about a uniform! Horatio Herbert, Lord Kitchener, sometimes enjoyed doing more with the men than watching them drill. When not engaged in these more civilized pleasures, the general occupied himself propping up the British Empire. Some of his little forays into the storied pages of history were the (unsuccessful) rescue of Gordon at Khartoum, the Battle of Omdurman, and of course, the Great War. Every inch the servant of Empire, he *did* perhaps make use of some rather dubious methods of dealing with the Boers. Like concentration camps. The gaudy spree that was his career ended when a German mine sent his ship to the bottom in 1916.

ne of the representative voices of the 1920s was Carl Van Vechten. He started out as a music and dance critic, and later produced several sparkling novels that still wear fairly well (*The Tattooed Countess, Nigger Heaven*). For those still reeling at that last-named title, rest assured that Van Vechten was no racist. Quite the contrary. He was an early promoter and cheerleader for black culture, one of the godfathers of the Harlem Renaissance. Later in his life he gave up all writing, and became a superb photographer. He was gay, though married to the diminutive actress Fania Marinoff.

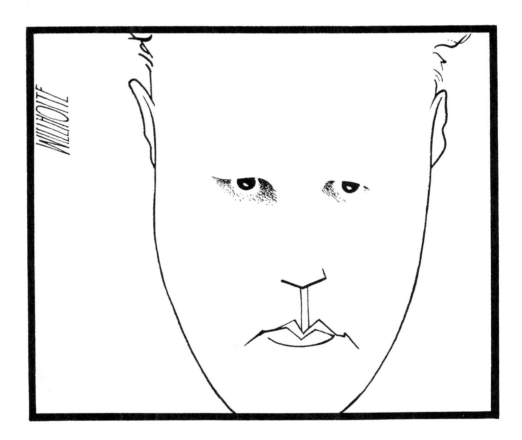

In contrast to, say, Millard Fillmore, who's almost *famous* for being obscure, James Buchanan was one of our more invisible presidents. (But let's allow that Lincoln, who followed him in office, would upstage *anybody*.) Buchanan started as a Federalist, but when that party disintegrated, he became a Democrat. The man had a fine legal mind, but not a scintilla of the moral courage required to stop slavery or even effect a decent compromise. Was it only contempt for his failures or his bachelorhood that led people to accuse him of being homosexual? Or maybe those tales about him and one-time vice president William Rufus Devane King were true...

Denton Welch led a miserable life, by any yardstick. Born in Shanghai to English parents, he was brought back to dear old Blighty to attend school. He started his studies in painting, but halfway through, while riding a bicycle along a country lane, he was hit and cruelly mangled. As a result of the accident, he began life anew as a writer. During his short life he published only two novels and a book of stories. All his others came out posthumously, notably *A Voice through a Cloud*, his great expression of pain. His wonderfully observant journals paint a vivid, unforgettable picture of Britain in the thirties and forties. In them, he's frank about his homosexuality, though it gave him little pleasure.

nteresting family, the Housmans. The three gay siblings were poet A.E. Housman, a lesbian sister Clemence, then Laurence. He was a sometime illustrator (e.g., of Christina Rossetti's sexually ambiguous *Goblin Market*), an indifferent poet, and all-around man of letters. His greatest fame came as a playwright, though he always seemed to fall afoul of the censors — on religious or political grounds. Even his great success *Victoria Regina* was kept off the London stage for three years, till in 1937 the British lifted their absurd ban on plays portraying the royal family. In the hiatus, it stormed Broadway, establishing Helen Hayes as a star of the first rank.

ir Arthur Seymour Sullivan,
Composer operettical,
Looked down on his more famous work
(An attitude heretical):
Those silly charming musicals that
Some discerning men adore,
Like *Iolanthe, Ruddigore* and
Gondoliers and *Pinafore.*
He much preferred his ponderous
Pretentious op'ra *Ivanhoe,*

A symphony, cantatas, and
A florid oratorio.
He hated Mr. Gilbert, so
He'd bite the bullet musical;
On ladies' eyes he'd rhapsodize
In manner most enthusical;
And that's the very reason for
The solemn look upon his face:
He was the very model of
A chicken-hearted closet case.

willhoite

On October 1975, Norman Scott, male model and professional sleazebag, cried to the papers that one Andrew Newton, on behalf of the Honorable Jeremy Thorpe, head of Britain's Liberal Party, had attempted to murder him. Thorpe, a diminutive punchinello, had been merrily humping young Scott. The trial was a carnival, with the British press in full — and gleeful — pursuit, but Thorpe was acquitted: the judge, in spite of damning love letters, never even put him on the stand. ("You must not assume that mere affection necessarily implies buggery.") There *were* consequences, however. Thorpe and Prime Minister Harold Wilson resigned, and Lord Snowdon, a friend of Thorpe, separated from Princess Margaret. Oh, those reserved British!

WILKHOLTE

Tall and raw-boned, handsome and elegant, Elizabeth Bowen was Anglo-Irish to the heart, and was by that fact politically divided. Though confident of her literary powers, she was shy and always suffered from a stammer. Her best-known books were novels, like *The Heat of the Day* and *The Death of the Heart*. But among the twenty-seven books she published in her lifetime were travel books, criticism, short stories, and history. The book closest to her heart was probably *Bowen's Court*, the story of her Irish estate. Appointed Commander of the British Empire in 1948, she was also awarded dozens of other honors. In 1973, cigarettes killed her but posthumous books kept coming: *Collected Stories, The Mulberry Tree...*

Nicolai Mikhailovitch Przhevalsky (say it three times — fast!) was a truly intrepid explorer. Not for him the dismal damps and tangled terrors of Mykonos, Key West, and Ibiza, *no*. Tibet! Mongolia! Singkiang! Siberia! He studied the flora and fauna (naming a wild horse for himself for good measure), extensively mapped the desolate eastern territories, and generally made himself useful to Russian exploration — and expansion. He always made sure to pack a little lovin' comfort as well. I mean, you know what those long nights in Siberia can be like...

In the Book of Truth it is written: thou shalt love thy neighbor as thyself; thou shalt do unto others as ye would have them do unto you; and, according to Francis Cardinal Spellman, thou shalt bomb the fucking hell out of the North Vietnamese. The hawkish cardinal was every bit the equal of some of today's churchmen (Jerry Falwell and Pat Robertson, say) in putting dubious political concerns before the Word of God. Those religious hypocrites are all alike, with one signal difference: Spellman is *said* to have been a regular at the boy brothels of New York. If that's not true, it must have been another cardinal who looked just like him.

would rather be a bright leaf on the stream of a dying civilization than a fertile seed dropped in the soil of a new era." Luscious Lucius Beebe must have seemed an odd duck among the modestly dressed masses. He was a time traveler from the Gilded Age, affecting mink-lined morning coat, derby, spats, and a diamond boutonniere. Sort of a Liberace with balls. So it was the height of the Depression? No matter. Style was everything. Like many a gay man before and since, he compensated for his good fortune by a flood of activity. Not only was he a newspaper columnist and drama critic, but he wrote books on the poet E.A. Robinson, trains, and a dozen other subjects.

Unfortunately, Karol Szymanowski's music is infrequently played today, even though he died as recently as 1937. Although his early music showed Russian, French, and German influences, his later work returned stylistically to the Polish. So perhaps he still thrills the souls of the musical Poles. He was prolific, too, composing a significant number of symphonies, chamber works, songs, and liturgical music. Every now and then, an American orchestra will put him on a program, but essentially, he doesn't travel well. Although travel to southern Italy was another thing entirely. The boys diving from the rocks, it's said, were his particular thing.

My candle burns at both ends; It will not last the night." Edna
St. Vincent Millay was a discharge of energy incarnate. A lyric
poet of great skill and quotability, she brought a new freshness to
the sonnet form. She also wrote stories and articles under the name
Nancy Boyd, and even tackled the theatre, as actress and director.
Her verse play *The King's Henchman* was turned into an opera by
Deems Taylor, so there was another world conquered. The era of
her great creativity was the 1920s, her demesne Greenwich Village.
There, her willowy pre-Raphaelite beauty easily seduced both men
and women. A not-of-this-world quality didn't hurt either. But she
guttered, and her flame flickered out early, at age fifty-eight.

Martin Green's *Children of the Sun* is a sardonic study of the Cambridge decadents of the 1920s. Precious Brian Howard, exquisite Guy Burgess, gorgeous Donald Maclean. *And* Harold Acton. A bright, pretty faun in his youth (and therefore *extremely* popular), he never lost his grace in maturity. Only his hair. A minor poet and accomplished writer on theatre and on Chinese art, he blossomed as a chronicler of Italian history and art, with an emphasis on the Renaissance. An intimate friend of Nancy Mitford (no, boys, not *that* intimate), he wrote a gracious memoir of her after her death. His own reminiscences, *Memoirs of an Aesthete* and *More Memoirs*, are worth a look, too.

William Plomer was born in South Africa to English parents. Sent to England to school, he returned with a certain polish — and a zest for literature. Farming in the back country provided him with the solitude to read, and started Plomer himself writing. An early novel, *Turbott Wolfe,* dealt with interracial love; the benighted South Africans were *not* charmed. So Plomer set out again, this time as a journalist, for Japan. He returned home only once, years later. Poetry, criticism, and librettos for several operas by Benjamin Britten solidified his literary reputation in England. It was a sweet life — made sweeter by a cloudless thirty-year love affair with Charles Erdman, a German refugee.

illie Maugham was *no* gentleman. In *Cakes and Ale*, an otherwise gentle comedy, the character Alroy Kear was a savage satire of Maugham's fellow novelist Hugh Walpole. Reading the book while dressing for dinner at a country house, Walpole couldn't put it down. The host, coming up to see why the novelist hadn't shown up, found him still standing at the mantel, horror-stricken but still reading, his pants fallen around his ankles. Walpole was a pretty good writer, indeed quite popular in his day, but hardly anyone reads him now. (Not unlike Maugham himself.) Although *Cakes and Ale* took rather a bite out of him, a knighthood four years before his death appeased him somewhat.

Plain and dowdy as a girl, oppressed by the Victorian fustian of her home, Elsie de Wolfe longed for a life with a little flair. She found it. A talent for amateur theatricals turned into a profession when her father's death left the family destitute. Even without a first-rate talent (as she herself realized), she was acclaimed as an actress — and as the best-dressed woman on the American stage. When her lover, agent Bessie Marbury, suggested that she channel her innate good taste into interior decoration, Elsie went for it, with a roaring success. She became a great international hostess — at Villa Trianon at Versailles, no less — and the wife of elderly Sir Charles Mendl. Flair, *indeed.*